Subways

by Allison Lassieur

Consultant:
James Anyansi
Public Affairs
New York Transit Authority

Bridgestone Books
an imprint of Capstone Press
Mankato, Minnesota

Bridgestone Books are published by Capstone Press
818 North Willow Street, Mankato, Minnesota 56001
http://www.capstone-press.com

Library of Congress Cataloging-in-Publication Data
Lassieur, Allison.
    Subways/by Allison Lassieur.
    p. cm.—(The Transportation library)
    Includes bibliographical references and index.
    Summary: Explores the world of subways, discussing their inventor and history,
how they work, what it is like to travel on them, and how early models compare with
modern ones.
    ISBN 0-7368-0364-5
    1. Subways—Juvenile literature. [1. Subways.] I. Title. II. Series.
TF845.L27 2000
388.4′28—DC21   99-24132
                                                                                                              CIP

Editorial Credits
Rebecca Glaser, editor; Timothy Halldin, cover designer; Heather Kindseth, illustrator;
  Kimberly Danger, photo researcher

Photo Credits
Archive Photos/Museum of the City of New York, 12
Cheryl Conlon, 18
Index Stock Imagery/K.J.B., 20
John Elk III, 6, 8
London Transport Museum, 8 (inset), 14, 14 (inset), 16
Mary Messenger, cover
Thomas Kitchin/Tom Stack and Associates, 4

Table of Contents

The Subway

A subway is an underground train system. A subway train carries people to different parts of a city. Subway trains sometimes travel on or above the ground for part of a trip. Subway trains that ride on elevated tracks are called Els.

elevated

above the ground

Traveling by Subway

Passengers board subway trains at subway stations. Here, passengers buy tokens or fare cards to pay for subway rides. They put the tokens or fare cards in slots on turnstiles. Passengers then board subway trains. Passengers stand if all the seats are filled.

turnstile

a gate with bars that lets only one person through at a time

train operator

windows

seats

metal pole

sliding doors

Parts of a Subway

Subway trains have several cars. Each subway car has sliding doors. Subway cars have many seats and large windows. Passengers hold on to metal poles when they stand. A train operator in the front car drives the subway train. Computers drive some subway trains.

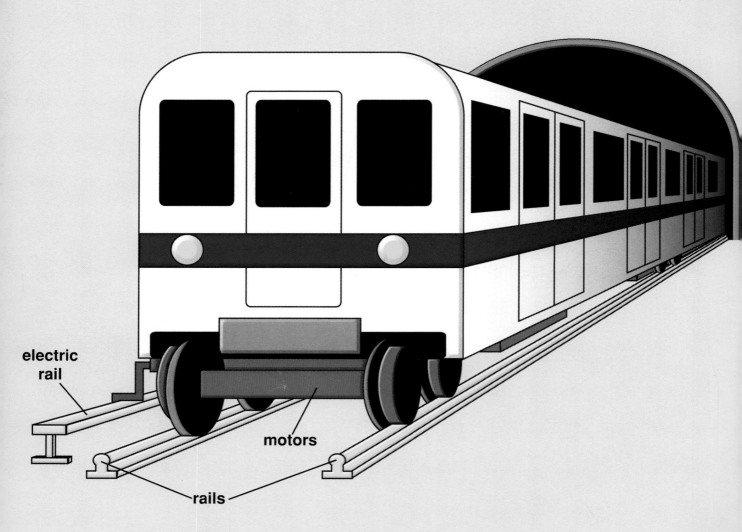

electric
rail

motors

rails

How a Subway Works

A subway train travels on two rails. The wheels roll on the rails. Electricity flows through a third rail beside the main rails. The electricity powers small motors under each subway car. The motors make the subway train move.

Before the Subway

People walked or traveled in horse-drawn carriages before the subway was invented. Travel from one part of a city to another took a long time. By the late 1800s, cities were crowded. They did not have enough space for trains.

carriage
a vehicle with wheels that usually is pulled by horses

The First Subway

Charles Pearson was a city planner in London. He had the idea to build an underground train system. Workers dug trenches. They built sides and a roof on the trenches. This building method is called cut-and-cover. The first subway opened in London in 1863.

trench

a long, narrow ditch in the ground; trenches form tunnels for subways

Early Subway Trains

Steam powered early subway trains. Subway workers burned coal to heat water. The heated water made steam. Steam-powered trains produced dark smoke from the coal fires. Smoke filled subway tunnels and made everything dirty.

Subways around the World

More than 50 cities around the world have subways. A few subway trains do not run on rails. They have rubber tires that run in narrow trenches. Montreal, Canada, and Paris, France, have this type of subway train.

Subway Facts

- More than four million passengers ride the New York City subway every day.

- In 1868, Alfred Beach built the first subway in New York City. The subway train did not have a motor. Big fans blew air into the tunnel to push the subway train.

- Subway trains in Tokyo, Japan, are very crowded. During busy times, more than 300 people may ride in one car.

- The subways in Mexico City, Mexico, and San Francisco, California, travel through tunnels built to stay up during earthquakes.

Hands On: Build a Model Subway Tunnel

Many subway tunnels are built using the cut-and-cover method. Workers cut a trench through an area. They then cover it with a roof. You can build your own cut-and-cover tunnel.

What You Need

A sandbox

A shoebox with a lid

A small shovel

Scissors

What You Do

1. Dig a trench in the sandbox. Make the trench deep enough to put the shoebox inside. Make the trench longer than the shoebox.
2. Cut off the ends of the shoebox.
3. Put the shoebox in the trench.
4. Put the lid on the shoebox.
5. Fill any spaces between the shoebox and the trench sides with sand. Cover the lid with sand.

The walls and lid of the shoebox are stronger than the sand. They hold up the tunnel roof. In a real subway tunnel, columns also help hold up the roof.

Words to Know

earthquake (URTH-kwayk)—a sudden shaking of the ground

electricity (e-lek-TRISS-uh-tee)—power; subways get power from an electric rail.

elevated (EL-uh-vay-ted)—something that is lifted above the ground

method (METH-uhd)—a way of doing things

token (TOH-kuhn)—a metal coin used in place of money; passengers buy tokens or fare cards to ride the subway.

Read More

Collicut, Paul. *This Train.* New York: Farrar, Straus & Giroux, 1999.

Hewett, Joan. *Tunnels, Tracks, and Trains: Building a Subway.* New York: Lodestar Books, 1995.

Stille, Darlene R. *Trains.* A True Book. New York: Children's Press, 1997.

Internet Sites

Garrett A. Morgan Transportation Wonderland
http://www.dot.gov/edu/k5/gamk5.htm
Metropolitan Transit Authority—New York
http://www.mta.nyc.ny.us
New York City Subway Resources
http://www.nycsubway.org

Index